T0072370

# The Pioneers' Story:
# Howell- Hickling

CAROLYN M. (SOPER) MIEHLE

**BALBOA**.PRESS
A DIVISION OF HAY HOUSE

Balboa Press books may be ordered through booksellers or by contacting:

Balboa Press
A Division of Hay House
1663 Liberty Drive
Bloomington, IN 47403
www.balboapress.com
844-682-1282

Because of the dynamic nature of the Internet, any web addresses or links contained in this book may have changed since publication and may no longer be valid. The views expressed in this work are solely those of the author and do not necessarily reflect the views of the publisher, and the publisher hereby disclaims any responsibility for them.

The author of this book does not dispense medical advice or prescribe the use of any technique as a form of treatment for physical, emotional, or medical problems without the advice of a physician, either directly or indirectly. The intent of the author is only to offer information of a general nature to help you in your quest for emotional and spiritual well-being. In the event you use any of the information in this book for yourself, which is your constitutional right, the author and the publisher assume no responsibility for your actions.

Any people depicted in stock imagery provided by Getty Images are models, and such images are being used for illustrative purposes only. Certain stock imagery © Getty Images.

Print information available on the last page.

ISBN: 979-8-7652-2601-8 (sc)
ISBN: 979-8-7652-2612-4 (e)

Balboa Press rev. date:  03/14/2022

# CONTENTS

# INTRODUCTION

The trials pioneers faced and endured, in a wild wilderness country come to life with the unfolding of family life. Many twists and turns, all experienced life with various talents and skills and above all, energy that is never ending.

The promise of land ownership drew multitudes of people from all cultures to northern Ontario through the Free Grants and Homestead Act of 1868. There was also the option to buy more, in 100-acre clumps, for 50 cents an acre. Some were also provided land grants through military service following the War of Independence 1775-1783.

The heartbreak of loss, as well as the joy of family celebrations built the strong sense of community, helping others making light of huge barn raisings, construction of churches, schools, lumbering and reforestation. All were carving out a new and better life for themselves and the generations to come. There were rewards for hard labour.

All these have the back drop of global events, wars, service to country, duty and dedication to causes greater than ourselves. Life just continues to unfold as it will.

# PREFACE

This is a tribute to the Howell and Hickling families, the author's maternal ancestry. All entries provided by members of the family have been identified and they were received with gratitude. They shared their perception as events impacted each of their lives from their unique points of view.

Every family has its own rich history. Hopefully this account will present, although incomplete, some insight into the lives of early pioneers in the "Near North".

Some hailing from Wales, *against* the loyalist cause, and some from England, fighting *for* the loyalist cause, in the 1770's, they wind their way, migrating gradually to Canada, homesteading in Prince Edward County, Oro, Stisted and Muskoka Districts, neighboring McMurrich. Utilizing rail service from Sprucedale, marketing in Huntsville and facilitating early lumbering and reforestation efforts in the area.

# CHAPTER 1

My father, Robert Soper, passed away February 6, 2001, a sudden heart attack after having his afternoon nap. He had planned a meeting with his friend to plan meals for their summer sailing trip on Georgian Bay that day, and when the friend phoned, Mom went upstairs to wake him and found him. He wore nitro pills around his neck and had been under doctor's care for the condition for a few years. This condition however, never deterred him from doing all the things he enjoyed, vacationing in Florida, travelling, lodge, canoeing and sailing. He lived his life to the fullest. Although missed by the entire family, the blessing was that it was the way he would have wished his end to come.

My husband, Frank Miehle and I, attended his funeral driving through quite a storm coming north from Niagara Falls, with our daughter and son-in-law. We stayed at the cottage on Bear Lake, a cold spot to be in February. After all was said and done, we stopped in to notify my uncle, my mother's brother, that Dad had passed away. Uncle Alex, 92 years of age, lived in Oakville and the trip would have been difficult for him and an extra load for our Mom, so he wasn't expected to attend.

We arrived at his home on Bronte Road in Oakville and walking in, found the home to be very cold, so cold you could see your breath. He was seated on his bench in the kitchen surrounded by an array of tools, dirty dishes, newspapers etc. piled on the small table.

He had always been rather eccentric so nothing surprised me.

We told him about Dad and upon leaving said casually, if there is anything we could help him with, to give us a call.

POA and executor duties, to act on his behalf, had been assigned to our Mom, Maudie, his sister. Unknown to me, she had informed him that his affairs would be too much for her to handle, since she lived up north and she was not as strong, as in the past and felt, at 81 years of age, she would be overwhelmed by his care and estate. He asked her who she had for herself and being told Sylvia, my sister and I, were to act on her behalf, he inquired if we were healthy enough to take on those responsibilities for him. She told him he would have to ask us. If we were willing and able, thankfully, it would relieve her of that worry and responsibility. That was the beginning of a long saga with Uncle Alex and the unfolding of many of the family stories.

The following year, Aunt Eva, our Mom and Uncle Alex's sister passed away, Sept. 22, 2002. She had been in a senior's home for a few years with severe mobility issues after a hip replacement. She had suffered from osteomyelitis, a bone disease since the age of eight.

Our Mom remembered being awakened by Eva's cry in the night, as a child, suffering from sudden extreme pain, as her left leg drew up tight to her body.

The condition in later years, caused a serious sway in her gait, eased, but not corrected, by the heavy lifts on the orthopedic shoe she wore. In spite of her years of difficulty, I remember that visiting her was a pleasure as she was always so positive about life and made everyone feel so welcome in her presence. She shared details of her life experience from her point of view, which will be included later in the text.

I called Uncle Alex to let him know that I would pick him up to give him a ride to her funeral in Huntsville and had arranged for him to stay with my sister, Maryne, in Port Sydney, just south of Huntsville. We had prearranged that she would get him cleaned up for the funeral the following day. I picked him up. Since he had lived alone for over 25 years, had lost his sense of smell, being clean was not a priority, along with the fact that he was incontinent, the odor of urine was prevalent. I was able to find his cleanest dirty shirt and put a few things in a bag for his stay with Maryne. I drove with the windows open most of the way.

Bless her, she and her husband, Rick got him bathed and cleaned up for the following day. He was thrilled with the attention and asked Sylvia and I, to take on his POA and executorship duties, if we were willing. We accepted and since I lived closer, I took on visiting him monthly to organize and understand the scope of the responsibility, with frequent calls for support and guidance from Sylvia.

Thus began the many discussions with Uncle Alex and the unfolding of the family history, told through his eyes. He had committed a great deal to paper, so many of the accounts are his, also the writings of Uncle Bill Howell, my great uncle, my grandmother, Jessie's youngest brother, both are accompanied by those parts I remember in the telling.

# CHAPTER 2

The union of Jessie Howell (1884-1955) and Andrew Hickling (1869-1939), married Dec. 25,1907, resulted in five children, Alex (1909), Muriel (1911), Hester (1916), Eva (1918) and **Maudie** (1920). (My maternal grandparents)

Great Grandma Hickling, Andrew's mother, lived up the road from their home and Alex said he wished his mother would stop going to his Grandma Hickling's because it seemed to him, being the first born, that every time she went up there, she came back with another baby. Each took the time and attention away from him which he did not appreciate at all. Great Grandma Hickling was a mid-wife and many in the community solicited her assistance. Hospital births were not possible due to distance and time to travel there by wagon.

The Hickling background, tracing the male line of my mother, Maudie's side:

My great great great grandfather, George Hickling:

Tracing the Hickling family tree takes us back to **George** Hickling (1770-1836) born near Loughborough, England, in Norwich County. He became a Baptist Minister and also apprenticed as a turner and patternmaker. He served in the Navy. He shows up again as a pioneer of Upper Canada, getting a land grant on the

Penetanguishene Road by Order of Counsel, passed in April 26, 1819.

There were six children born in his marriage to Elizabeth Denston: Eliza(Drury), George Jr.(1802), William(1806-1892),Ebenezer(?), **John**(1815-1887), and Charles(1817-1909). George Sr. was alotted Lot 15 on concession 1 in Oro. Elizabeth Denston never left England to join her husband so how and when some or all of the children ended up in Canada is a mystery. As adults, George Jr. homesteaded on lot 52, Oro. Ebenezer settled on lot 19, concession 2, Oro. Charles came in 1831 and lived in the Penetang settlement. Eliza married Edmund Drury of Vespra.

My great great grandfather John Hickling (1815-1887): **John**(1815-1887)). He married Jane Kneeshaw and there were three children from this union. **Alexander**(1840-1925), John Jr.(?), and Mary Eliza(?) married Joseph Henry Oades in 1864 and moved to Nebraska

My great grandfather Alexander Hickling (1840-1925) married Catharine McNabb (1846-1923) in 1866.

The **Alexander** (1840-1925) Hickling family came north to Muskoka, from Elmhurst and Oro, just north of Barrie. He worked in a sawmill on the Penetanguishene Road. He wanted to purchase a farm there, however the prices were too high, so he homesteaded in Muskoka, Stisted township. He came to Yearley alone, walking, and led a pregnant heifer and carried his ax and saws. He built a shack and stayed there over winter, after locating 200 acres, lots 8 and 9 on Concession 12, under the Free Grants Act in 1877.

John Graves Simcoe had opened up the Muskoka area for settlement. Alexander had no problem finding enough to eat as he dug up roots and snared rabbits and hunted game, prevalent in the area. In 1878 he went back to Oro and returned with his wife, Catherine McNabb (1846-1923) and two boys, Jack, ten years old and **Andrew**, eight years old, walking all the way. **Andrew** was Uncle Alex and **Maudie**'s father.

On the return trip Catharine noticed a market in Huntsville and with her business sense, decided to sell butter and eggs there. She strapped a wooden box to her back to hold the butter and eggs and made the trip to Huntsville every Saturday, walking a distance of 26 km or 16 miles. They started then to build a log house. They also cleared land for farming.

Catharine returned to Oro, after contacting her brother, to locate a horse and buggy. Her brother found what his sister wanted and she walked to Oro, bringing back the horse and buggy to facilitate her weekly trips to the Huntsville market. This was their main source of income.

Alexander and Catharine had five children in all, John Henry (1867-1940), **Andrew** (1869-1939), Alexander (1880-1881), Maude (Hines) (1881-1965), and Mabel (Liddard)(1886-1928).

Andrew at age 14 wanted to go out west to earn money bringing in the harvest. His elder brother, Jack and Joe Middleton were both permitted to go as they were 16. Catherine, their mother told Andrew that she had other plans for him. She told him that if he went to work in the lumber camp, that she was sure he would end up with the same amount of money as his brother, Jack, when he returned from the west. Listening to his mother, he worked in the lumber camps from the age of 14 to the age of 38.

His mother urged him to deposit all his pay checks in the bank and when he wanted to purchase something to discuss it with her since she made weekly trips to Huntsville and she could compare prices and assure him regarding the best buys.

Andrew's brother John Henry Hickling, homesteaded across the road from Andrew and Jessie's place and their children grew up together.

John married Annie Blundel and they had three children, Ivy,

Hazel and Winnifred. They carried and lost four more children which was common during those times with hospitals so far away.

Catherine, Alexander's wife, in her later years, developed "dropsy" and passed away Nov. 11, 1923. Jessie cared for her mother-in-law at night and Alexander, her husband, cared for her during the day. Jessie's children were unaccustomed to seeing their mother sleeping during the day, requiring them to fare for themselves.

When the townships of McMurrich and Stisted first opened up, people of widely different nationalities rushed in to settle and were influenced in their selection of location by the nationality of those already there. Thus Irish, Scottish, English, German, and later, Italian and Finnish settled in different sections of the townships.

According to Uncle Alex notes, he writes,
"What Grandpa Hickling (Alexander) Said…
"The earliest episodes I recall Grandpa Alex Hickling telling me about, occurred on the Penetang Road near Dalston where he worked in a sawmill and framed barns. He never mentioned a rate of pay in the sawmill but said he was paid $27 dollars for framing a barn, large or small. The farmer would deliver the logs to the site and Grandpa would square the logs, preparing them cut to lengths, drill and brace each corner, and prepare all the joints for assembly. Then the farmer would call the neighbours for a barn raising. Grandpa would oversee the raising operation. His job was complete when the timbers were in place and the rafters were on. Usually, the farmer would nail the barn boards himself."

Barn raising bees were something to look forward to as there would be a feast and dance that followed, to celebrate. Food was plentiful since there were no game laws. Fur trappers reaped a rich harvest from beaver, wolves, wild cats, deer, moose, lynx etc. Everyone contributed to the festivities. Square dancing to a caller

*Carolyn M. (Soper) Miehle*

accompanied by fiddle music, guitars and perhaps a banjo. Waltzes were always a favourite.

He continues to write,

"Grandpa was born in 1840 and Grandma in 1846, and married in 1865, in Barrie. The story goes that once wed, Grandpa had a boiler maker and Grandma had a hot toddy. Both fell asleep and upon awakening, the twenty-seven dollars he had were gone. She told him he could not manage money therefore she decided to manage their money for the future. Grandpa later reported that that was the best decision they made as she watched every penny."

# CHAPTER 3

My grandfather, Andrew Hickling (1869-1939):

**Andrew Hickling** (1869-1939) and **Jessie Howell** (1884-1955), **Maudie's** parents, were married Dec.25 1907, when he came home from the lumber camp for Christmas, returning the next day. Fifteen years her senior, Andrew said he had to wait for her to grow up so he could marry her.

With $3000 in the bank, Andrew felt he had enough to live on and turned to clearing and working the land, rather than working in the camps.

At the time they cut all the hay using scythes. The first cut would be made by Alex, then Jack, then Andrew, one following the other. Andrew heard of mowers and purchased one, the first in the area. All the neighbours came to see it and the following year Andrew sold it to a neighbour and purchased another. So it went that he "dealt" mowers, being fascinated with any motorized equipment. He was viewed as an innovator in the area.

**Andrew** Hickling, father to Alex, Muriel, Hester, Eva and **Maudie**, was fifteen years older than his wife, Jessie. He passed away, Dec,13,1939, one month after the double wedding of two of their daughters, Eva and Maudie.

I, Carolyn (1946), one of Maudie's daughters, can remember Grandma Jessie (Howell) Hickling (1884-1955). Her warm kitchen, the peppermint candies she had in a jar on the window sill, the aroma of fresh bread and her warm loving arms are easily brought to mind. I was nine when she passed away. She was an amazing woman.

The Jessie Howell family ancestry will be disclosed, later in the story, as it, also had many twists and turns.

Andrew Hickling worked in the lumber camps so Jessie, his wife, was on her own with the children much of the time.

Uncle Alex continues writing,

"My earliest recollections of being home alone were with only Mom, Muriel and myself. Pop would be in the lumber camp. Mom would be sitting in front of the stove with her feet on the oven door and she would always be knitting something. Muriel and I would be wrestling on the mat. I think now I must have resented Muriel for coming between Mom and me, long before I can remember. Since I was sickly for the first year or so of my life, I had had my Mom's undivided attention.

Muriel was 13 lbs when she was born and never stopped growing. She used to tell me she was bigger than me and stronger than me and could take me down any day of the week. One time I was holding her down and she became frantic and bit my arm, enough to show teeth marks but not break the skin. I cried and ran to Mom but she gave me very little sympathy. When more babies came, we both tried to win them over to our side of the fence. Because they were girls or maybe because Muriel tried harder, she won most of the time. Also, I was more interested in bicycles than dolls.

By the time I was 8 or 10 it was my job to feed and water the cattle after school. Muriel carried in the firewood from the woodshed to the house.

Occasionally Mom would get a phone call that the police were coming and she would send me over to warn Jim Middleton." (perhaps to check on moonshine operations.)

Jessie being a clever business woman, made an arrangement with Jim Middleton. He was frequently short of cash so she arranged perhaps one of the first reverse mortgages. He agreed to a price for his property and when in need of money would make a draw on his account with Jessie. He lived the rest of his life on his property, visiting Jessie for cash and in the end the property was hers.

Uncle Alex continues,

"One night I had just finished the chores and was returning from the barn and I heard Grandpa Hickling hollering from the bush. I called Mom to come and listen and she sent me back to see if he needed help. I found Grandpa Hickling with a broken leg and under the sloop. He told me to get Billy Usher to come and help him. Between us, we got him out and onto the sleigh and up to Grandma's house. If I hadn't heard him hollering, he would likely have frozen to death.

Floss and Jewel were just colts then and they were brought down to our barn and I tended to them from then on.

I was probably about 11 or so then. I was gradually allowed to hitch the horses and do some ploughing and harrowing after that. When I was allowed to take the horses on the road, I was 14 and my first trip was to Buck Lake, Saturday afternoon. Pop was working on the river drive so I would bring him home for Sunday."

(Incidentally, he worked the river drive and could not swim.)

Andrew Hickling was a respected member of the community and a very supportive father.

A classic Canadian and American tradition- log driving is depicted by the vignette on utube: View the feats of log drivers.... amazing.

The Log Driver's Waltz by John Weldon, National Film Board of Canada.

1)"If you ask any girl from the parish around, what pleases her most from her head to her toes? She'll say, "I'm not sure if it's business of yours, but I do like to waltz with a log driver."

Chorus:

*Carolyn M. (Soper) Miehle*

For he goes burlin' down and down white water, that's where the log driver learns to step lightly. It's burlin' down and down white water, the log driver's waltz pleases girls completely.

2)When the drive's daily is over, I like to go down and watch all the lads as they work on the river. I know that come evenin' they'll be in the town, and we all like to waltz with a log driver.

3)To please both my parents, I've had to give way and dance with doctors and merchants and lawyers. Their manners are fine, but their feet are of clay, but there's none with the style of my log driver.

4)Now I've had my chances with all sorts of men, but none is so fine as my lad on the river. So when the drives over, if he asks me again, I think I will marry my log driver."

# CHAPTER 4

The children of Andrew Hickling and Jessie Howell: Alex, Muriel, Hester, Eva and Maudie:

Alexander Lorenzo Hickling (1909-2008): aka Jack Henry:

Uncle Alex was the first born to Andrew and Jessie Hickling: The entire story would be remiss if an account of Uncle Alex's life was omitted. Every family has a scallywag and Alex was ours. He fathered a child with a neighbour and thus disgracing the family was told by his father to "never darken their door again".

Fortunately, the Wreggitt family raised Elsie to be a fine individual in a loving home with wonderful family support. As a teenager, Alex went out west with his uncle, Bill Howell to the harvest. He later joined the army and enjoyed the camaraderie of his mates. He reported that they were scheduled to go overseas and it was decided that he had a German affiliation, with the name of Hickling and was separated from his unit. He found this to be very unfair and went a.w.o.l. from the army.

There is a German connection, however it is on Grandma Howell's side, her grandfather Nathan's second wife, Marion Best.

Alex's sisters recall police coming to Yearley, looking for their brother, who had disappeared. It was at this time he went under the radar and assumed the names of his two grandfathers and became Jack Henry. Under this name he met and married Bridget Elena

Carolyn M. (Soper) Miehle

Ryan, "Lena" in 1946. He was employed on farms in the Barrie area when they met.

He had an entrepreneurial spirit early in life:
Uncle Bill Howell writes,

"A school teacher came to Yearley and at the beginning of the school year asked who was to light the fire if she didn't want to. She devised a plan in which one of the children could earn money taking on the duty of lighting the fire and sweeping the school room floor. With parental consent, the students could sign up and he or she would have to have "smoke coming out of the chimney by 8 am" when the teacher would look out the window from down the road, to check. The school room then would be comfortable for 8:45 when she would arrive. Students would earn 10 cents a day for a fire and 5 cents for sweeping the floor. All wanted to try, the list was alphabetical. Alex bugged and bugged his father, Andrew for consent, until he finally agreed. He wanted Alex to practice at home. First, he would watch his father and the next day he would watch his son. One needed to make their own shavings, wrap them in paper and split their own wood. Alex's friend Johnny Usher didn't like lighting the fire and felt he could do better trapping. Rabbits brought 50 cents, weasel $1.50, and muskrat $2.50. He usually caught something every day. Many others dropped out of the program, giving Alex more days. Soon he had $10 saved. This grew to $25 and eventually he was the only one with the responsibility."

Alex and his wife, Lena lived in a trailer and while on the highway heading to Toronto, had a flat tire in Oakville and drove into a garage to have it repaired. The garage proprietor allowed them to park their trailer on his lot and Alex, "Jack" overheard that they were in need of carpenter apprentices.

He went to inquire and thus began his career as a carpenter. He continued in that trade until he recognized the need for a pension and was employed as a cleaner with the school board, qualifying for an OMERS pension that served him for the rest of his life.

He built a block home on property on Bronte Road which was way out in the country at the time. Here he lived the rest of his life until moving to a senior's home on Lakeshore Road. He was quite a savvy investment and money manager and was extremely "tight".

He was approached by the Seventh Day Adventist Church to sell his large property to them for the construction of their church. He thought it over and came up with an arrangement, he was in his 70's at the time. The deal was that they could buy his property provided that he could live in his house, until he died, in the meantime, they were to pay all the taxes and maintain the entire property, summer and winter. He lived to be 99. The house has been taken down and the church stands behind the cement platform where his home stood, 2031 Bronte Road, Oakville.

As one of his POA's, I visited him once a month to help him out, driving him on errands. He offered to take me out for lunch and to my surprise, his choice was Harvey's. All the following occasions, he seemed to have always forgotten his wallet. It was just who he was. Living through the depression, made spending any money, very difficult for him.

He even insisted that they shop around for inexpensive funeral arrangements and selected, "Just Cremation" for his future, in Burlington. He also suggested that since Lena had passed away so many years before that he could be buried in her plot, freeing up his space, which he felt I could get a "pretty penny" for, as cemetery plots had increased so much over the years. I told him I would think it over, and ultimately, he was buried in his own space next to his wife.

He had to have a hip replacement, his well went dry and the house was condemned. It was then I was able to persuade him to enter an assisted living facility, near the senior center that he frequented often. He later passed away at the Village of Tansley

Woods in Oakville. He was interred at the cemetery on Trafalgar Road.

While in the seniors home he wrote,

"Dear Carolyn,

This is a serious letter and I'm asking you for a serious response on a serious question. Take all the time you need to think it over and come to a long-term opinion. Shortly after my sisters died, I started getting visits from them at nights, often several of them would come together and sometimes separately. We didn't discuss the reasons for the visits, but they were always enjoyable. We rarely got into serious discussions about them but after they left, there remained questions in my mind about how they arrived and how they left. For example, they never said, "We're leaving now." They just disappeared. They never showed up at mealtime and were never around when bedtime came. They never asked me to write to them or discussed when they would be back. Muriel always came alone and she was still coming six months after she started coming. Maudie and Eva didn't continue the visits as long as Muriel. Maudie and Eva continued the visits for about three months. Hester didn't come at all, but she was a quiet girl and not as gushy as Maudie and Eva and possibly not so "attention getting" as Maudie and Eva. I tried to treat them all with a great deal of respect but they were all so different. It's not so easy to do. I just do the best I can. I hope they will understand. I will continue this letter later as I am not near finished yet. More will be forthcoming. I will take off for now and let you get started thinking about it. I call this letter Serious Letter #1, to be continued."

Serious Letter #2 never arrived... In thinking it over, it is a comfort to know that perhaps his sisters could visit him briefly coming through the veil or did he venture through the veil to visit them? Either way, it is wonderful he had this comfort from his sisters after they had passed away. It has been recorded, that astral voyages are possible, so perhaps he had that experience.

Letters he wrote and failed to post were found in his personal effects:

April 29, 2003, He writes,

"Dear Elsie, Many thanks for your letter. Very sorry to hear about your fall. I guess that ends your dancing anyway. I don't ever think of dancing anymore. I have to walk, the best I can do is to get to a McDonald's. My head is really my worst problem. I can't think or remember anything anymore. I'll put on one sock and forget to put on the other one. Yes, I still go out three days for dinner, Tues. Wed. and Thurs. Dinner, cards and exercises which I enjoy. I hardly limp at all now. I am really glad I quit driving. There are too many things to watch. A friend of mine was killed in a car accident last year. We become unconscious to having so many things to watch. We just can't do it anymore. So, I'm still alive yet. I need to have some way of suicide so I could die when I want to. I know its bearable when you have no pain but if I was in pain, I would want to be able to suicide when I wanted to escape the pain…"

Elsie was his daughter, so it seems they corresponded over the years and apparently, she also visited him at his home and while he was in the senior residence. He never spoke of her.

December 20, 2003, He writes,

"Dear Ellen,

My time seems to be running out. However, Maudie's daughter Carolyn moved me from my house to a Seniors Center in Oakville where I get three meals a day, a warm room and a hot bath and no work. I hope to go back to my house in the spring. My eyesight and hearing are getting worse. My breathing bothers me a bit too, so don't be surprised if you see my name in the paper. It has been an honor to know you. Love from Alex."

Every visit with him was an adventure one never knew what to expect. He stayed alert until the end. A stroke took him to join his sisters in 2008 at the age of 99.

# CHAPTER 5

## The Girls of the Hickling Family

Muriel Hickling-Mattice (1911-1989):

Uncle Alex, (aka Jack Henry) shared memories of his sister, Muriel (1911-1989). Muriel was the second born to Andrew and Jessie.

"Muriel left home when she was 14 or perhaps, I should say she went to Toronto to help Auntie Mabel look after her children. Muriel and Aunty Mabel got along really well. Later, Mabel got her a job doing housework near her home. Sometimes Melbourne (Howell) would run square dances which Muriel attended and there she met Earl Silk from Huntsville, but working in Toronto, driving a lumber truck.

They married when Muriel was 17, I guess, and he was 30 or so. He was a steady worker but drank a lot, beat her and would go out with any woman that would go with him. So, Muriel put up with him for 2 years or so, then she paid $400 for a divorce which she paid for herself. She'd be making about $10-$20 per month so I guess it took her a few years to pay for it. Muriel worked as a live-in maid in a number of places after she left Earl, and each time he would find her and make such a fuss that she would lose her job. Finally, the last place she worked, she alerted the lady of the house of her situation and she said that she would handle everything for her, should he appear. Sure enough, Earl found her and the lady of the house told him that she also wanted to know her location, telling him that Muriel had taken off without notice, leaving her in quite a predicament. Earl believed the story and Muriel, in the house at the time, was spared further embarrassment. Then she married Jimmy Mattice."

They together adopted two children, Beulah and Rex and fostered Marie West.

James Mattice had been a confirmed bachelor and lived on the second concession in McMurrich township, quite close to the farm where I grew up.

Neighbours, Ted and Edna Black spoke highly of Uncle Jim as they first encountered him when they moved up to McMurrich. Their farm and home was next to his property. It was winter and both of them were very chilled with their travels north. Seeing that, he invited them into his home, rough and basic, and Edna said he served them the best bacon and eggs she had ever eaten, the night of their arrival. It was the way of the north. Neighbours would always help neighbours.

In their later years Aunt Muriel and Uncle Jim lived in a senior apartment in Huntsville on Brunel Road. Aunt Muriel had a heart attack, while laughing, during a card game with her friends and passed away shortly after. Uncle Jim survived her and suffering from dementia, passing away a month later.

Hester Hickling-Herckimer (1916-1982):
Uncle Alex writes about his second sister, Hester, third born to Andrew and Jessie.

"Hester (1916-1982) was quiet and more reserved than the rest of us, and seemed to prefer the company of women older than herself, eg. Alice Thurman, Nora Howell and Kate Godfrey. If I had been a better leader, perhaps it may have helped a lot."

Hester always had a sense of the finer side of life and tried to provide a small example, sharing her ideas with the family. She came home on a weekend from the city and offered to prepare a meal for her parents and siblings. She decked the table with white tablecloth, surplus cutlery, napkins etc. She also introduced something completely new, creamy mashed potatoes. Her father did not approve, as he felt potatoes should never be eaten that way and they never appeared again in the household.

Change is always a challenge to accept, even the small things.

Hester was a great help to Alex, on many occasions. She was the exception in the family. Since furthering her education was very important to her, she worked for her room and board in Huntsville and attended high school. She seemed destined for city life.

As her niece, I recall their frequent visits to our farm in Haldane Hill, driving up from Toronto and we all looked forward to them coming. She invited each of us, to visit her in Toronto, during our summer holidays and she exposed us to the wonder of Eaton's Center, the Ex., streetcars, subways and the bustle of the city. For a child, it was a wonderful experience.

She was married to Harold Herckimer, raising three children, Patricia (1942), Harold's daughter and their daughters Shirley (1952) and Nancy (1959). She was a good sport with camping and supporting Harold's love of fishing.

She was a devoted employee of the bank and was employed there when the Imperial Bank and Commerce Bank amalgamated, becoming CIBC. She was also a gifted cook and baker. Her table was always decked out with white linen tablecloth, cloth napkins, fancy dishes, a great deal of cutlery, decadent cakes on pedestal stands and eating was a festive occasion.

She was generous beyond description and boarded both of my sisters when they first went to the city. Tragically, she was killed by a motorcyclist as she got off the bus, coming home from work, in Oct. 1982. Harold survived her by four years and passed away in 1986.

Eva Hickling-Hunter (1918-2002):
Fourth child born to Andrew and Jessie:

Uncle Alex writes about his two youngest sisters, "I don't believe Maudie or Eva ever made an enemy in their entire lives." Eva (1918-2002) As a very young child, her Mother, Jessie, asked her to go and wake up her brother, Alex. Eva returned tearfully to her mother saying, "I sayed to Alex and sayed to Alex and Alex never sayed to me."

Maudie, asked her sister, Eva to write her life story and, Eva wrote,

"At the age of eight Eva was in severe pain as her left leg drew up tight to her body. Dr. Kitt from Sprucedale was called. She was confined to her bed for six weeks while arrangements were made for her to go to Orillia Memorial Hospital. Eva was taken by horse and sleigh to Sprucedale Station and there boarded and travelled by train in a baggage coach to Scotia. She was lying in a bed covered with pillows and quilts. Her parents and Dr. Kitt were with her. Dr. Kitt phoned Orillia from Scotia for an ambulance to meet them and take her to the hospital. Her father continued with them in Huntsville and her mother had to return to stay with the other children.

Two x-rays were taken and while under sedation her left leg was straightened and her hips and body were put in a plaster cast. A heavy weight was attached to her leg to keep it in position with sandbags on each side. Tests proved Eva had osteomyelitis. She was in hospital for six weeks.

Pa brought her home by train to Martin Siding and Alex, her brother met them with the horses and sleigh. She was in the cast for six months, then gradually began to get around, first in a wheelchair and later with crutches. Eva attended school on crutches and many times her brother, Alex would push her there in the wheelbarrow."

During the school day, on occasion, an airplane would fly over. At this time of history, that event was significant and the teacher would quickly usher all the children outside to view this special opportunity. This would have been in the 1920's. Airplanes were a real novelty.

Eva continues,

"At 21, November 4, 1939, Eva married Frank Hunter (1911-1998) from Huntsville, in a double wedding with her sister, Maudie and Bob Soper from Haldane Hill. Eva and Frank had three sons, Gordon, Roy and David.

In 1969, Eva had a complete hip replacement. Formerly all hospital bills were paid by the family, but Ontario Hospitalization Plans had been brought in by the government so she could have the surgery. The operation was a complete success."

Eva really enjoyed letter writing and corresponded with many people sharing her positive outlook on life.

Her sister, Maudie writes in 1991,

"I asked my sister Eva, to write a story of her life so I could include it in the family history book. I found it interesting and thought others might too.

I notice she left out the one thing which was probably the saddest of her life, and still hurts too much to write about…she lost her youngest son, David Ross, aged 35, with cancer. We all share her sorrow. Through all her early life of sickness, she remained cheerful always. She was, and still is, a bright light shining in, an often, dark world. We all love her very much."

Florence Maude Hickling-Soper (1920-2003):
Fifth child born to Andrew and Jessie:
**Maudie** (1920-2003), the youngest of the Andrew and Jessie Hickling family, married Bob Soper (1917-2001), Nov. 4, 1939. They had five children, Sylvia (1941), Robert (1943), Maryne (1945-2016), Carolyn (1946) and Mark (1965).

Uncle Alex writes about his sister, Maudie (1920-2003), "I don't know what Maudie did, but whatever she did, raising her family, it was the right thing as they all seemed to have turned out ok … Maudie had a lot of good luck, 1. She met Bob. 2. Soper family. 3. Bob's eyes prevented him from becoming a flyer in the Air Force and likely saved his life. 4. Maudie's personality produced five charming personalities plus good judgment for five. 5. You could fill a page with what you know of them… I join my parents in complimenting Maudie as being the most successful member of our family. Love Alex."

Alex continues,

"Ellen Tibby and Maudie had considered joining the army as war was approaching. Maudie, however was engaged to Gilbert Hopcraft. Bob was dating Beth Cousins at the time, a girl his parents didn't find suitable for him. Wearing Gilbert's ring didn't stop Bob from successfully wooing Maudie. Bob's parents felt Maudie was a good choice."

Maudie always accompanied her husband, living at first in a trailer that was parked near the Pig and Whistle in Sunnyside, when he worked in Toronto as a machinist. Sylvia and Bob Jr came along soon after and Maudie followed Bob, with children in tow from camp to camp. During the war, he served in the Air Force, initially stationed in Port Stanley, and later, in Belleville, where Maryne was born, then went overseas to Newfoundland, not yet a province, joining Canada in 1949.

After the war, they returned as a family to the Soper farm, in Haldane Hill, south of Sprucedale, the location of his parents' George and Grace Soper's former fox farm, (See: The British Immigrant's Story: Nothing Came Easy).

They lived at the farm when I was born in 1946. Mark came along in 1965, just as they were about to move to the Provincial Girl Guide Camp on Doe Lake, where Bob worked until his retirement.

They, then moved to Burk's Falls, purchasing a home on the Magnetawan River below the falls. Mark grew up on the Guide Camp and in Burk's Falls.

More on the Soper family later in the text.

# CHAPTER 6

The Howell ancestry dates back to 1700's.

Hugh Howell (1695-1745) father of Richard Howell (1714-1756) born in Cardiff, Wales.

Richard Howell married Ann Daniels in 1737 and they had 6 children. One of whom was John. (Sr.)

John was born in Sussex, New Jersey in 1753. He passed away 25 August 1820, in Sophiaburg, Prince Edward, Ontario.

John Howell Sr. (1753-1820) married Eva Catharine Sheets (1755-1798) and there were 9 children born in this union. Records show a second wife, Nancy Anne Fairman (1776-1844). Due to dates and births, it may be surmised that Eva died at the age of 43, perhaps in child birth, since the birth date of the last child coincides with the year 1798. The 7$^{th}$ and 8$^{th}$ were twins in 1796. Nancy would have been 22 years of age, while John was 45 at the time of the second marriage. There were no children of record with the second marriage.

His military rank in the army was that of Sergeant Major.

From "Settlement of Upper Canada" by Canniff, Mika Publishing Co.

"John Howell, a son of Richard Howell, was born in New Jersey in 1753."

"Settlement of Upper Canada, continues:

When 24 years old, John took up residence at Johntown on the Mohawk River. At the commencements of hostilities in 1776, (called the United States War of Independence from Britian, 1775-1783) he joined Sir John Johnson's 2nd Battalion and was raised to the position of Sergeant-Major. His name appears as such on the battalion roll, now before the writer. He remained in the army during the war, doing duties at St. John's Coteau du Lac, and many other places. When his company was disbanded at Oswego, in 1782, he came immediately to Kingston and thence to Fredericksburgh, where he settled upon his lot of 200 acres. By adhering to the loyal cause, Sergeant Howell suffered severe loss in real estate. The pleasant town of Rome(New York State) now stands upon the land which was his. His valuable property was not yielded up to the rapacious rebels without a legal effort to recover possession. The case was in court for many years, and Sergeant Howell spent $1400 in vain efforts to recover. No doubt it was pre-judged before he spent his money.

An event in Howell's life during the war is not without a touching interest. Before joining his regiment, he had courted and won the heart of a fair lady at Johnstown, a full-blooded Mohawk lady. While stationed at Coteau du Lac, he obtained permission during the winter, when hostilities subsided, to go to Johnstown to obtain his bride. Guided by seven Indians he set out to traverse a pathless wilderness, on snowshoes. The wedding trip had its perils and almost a fatal termination. On their return they lost their way in the interminable woods and soon found themselves destitute of food. For days they were without anything to eat. One day they shot a squirrel, which divided among them was hardly a taste for each. The thongs of their shoes were roasted and eaten, to allay the pangs of hunger. At last, they shot a deer, which had well-nigh proved the death of some, from over-eating. Two of the men were left behind, but they subsequently came in.

Sergeant Howell's loss as a loyalist was great: but, so far as could be, it was made good by Government. He drew 1,220 acres of land as an officer, and the same quantity for his family. At an early date after his arrival at the Bay, he was appointed Commissioner in the Peace, and subsequently he was made Colonel of the Prince Edward Militia. Soon after settling in Fredericksburgh, he built a windmill, opposite the Upper Gap, and probably the first mill built by an individual in the province. He afterwards sold it to one Russell, an Engineer in Kingston. The remains are still on the spot. He was a man of liberal education for the times, and was conversant with Dutch and French languages, and understood the Indian dialect. From his connection with the Johnstown settlement upon the Mohawk River, and his close contiguity to the Mohawk Indians upon the Bay, he held a high place in their regard. He often visited them and their chiefs as often, paid him state visits. They often called upon him to settle disputes, which he never failed to do by his sternness and kindness combined. His presence was sufficient to inspire awe amongst them, when disposed to be troublesome, which was increased by his long sword which he would hang to his side."

Uncle Bill Howell writes of the wedding trip experience, as told to him by Lorenzo, his father:

"Lorenzo told me of the trip with the Indians and of their extreme hunger. He said it was their leather military harness they "stewed". The "fair lady" was a full- blooded Mohawk Indian...the Indian features were very strong in my first cousins once removed. i.e. Charlie Howell of Orillia and ones at Tillsonburg. I have counted 52 first cousins. Johnson's had 11 children."

**John** Howell Jr. born in late 1780's, was father to **Nathan** Howell born 1813, John Jr. being my great- great-great grandfather.

Uncle Bill Howell writes about Lorenzo's grandfather, John Jr.

"Lorenzo's father was Nathan Howell and his mother Marion Best, they are both buried in the Best cemetery not far from Corinth." Nathan's father was John Jr., and one of the sons of John Sr. The trail being Hugh, Richard, John Sr., John Jr., Nathan, Lorenzo and then, my grandmother, Jessie Howell.

"The Howell, Howel, Howelle's and original spelling Huyld are all the same batch and were very prominent in repelling the Norsemens' invasions. They were strong on revolution against England and any with those names were caught in England in the 17th century were taken into the Tower of London for laryngitis operations. There were no failures."

The writer finds it interesting that historically, the Howell clan were anti-loyalists while in Wales and the following generations became strong loyalists in North America.

An interesting example of a change in beliefs. A belief is just a thought one keeps thinking and when free to make one's own choice, a shift is possible due to changing circumstances and new environments. Different experiences away from those entrenched in one place, give birth to new perceptions, judgements and actions and alliances.

Uncle Bill Howell writes of his grandfather, Nathan

"**Nathan** (1801-1878), first married an English girl, named Veitch, they had three daughters and two sons, their first son, Nathan was killed in the Boer War and Henry is related to all the Orillia Howells. The girls were Tamsen, Isabelle and Jane.

Nathan's first wife died and he remarried a German girl, Marion Best. Her family were proud of three things, first they were Bests, second, they were German and third, they were wealthy. Marion Best was good and kind to her step-children. She and Nathan had seven children together, Lewis, John, Elisha, Margaret, **Lorenzo**, Allan and Alice. (12 in total, children and step-children)

Her people visited from Pennsylvania and took Lorenzo, Allan and their cousin Jim Crane back to Pennsylvania and educated them. Lorenzo was 21 when he returned... Jim Crane started Crane Enterprises in Aylmer.

Lorenzo remembered when getting in trouble he would run to his step brothers and sisters for support and they were a very close family"

# CHAPTER 7

**Lorenzo** Howell (1850-1929) married Mary Jane Staples (1861-1934), March 21, 1881

There were eight children born of this union. Hester (1882-1897), **Jessie** (1884-1955), Melbourne (1886-1952), Laurie (1888-1889), Florence (1892-1955), Stanley (1894-1897), Nora (1899-1942), William (1904-1986).

Mary Jane Staples' parents were Duncan Staples and Sarah Ann Mallough, parents to four girls; Mary Jane, Elizabeth, Annie and Sarah.

Written by my grandmother, Jessie Howell, about her mother, Mary Jane Staples' upbringing:

"Duncan Staples born at Queenston Heights, (Niagara), was Mary Jane's father and Sarah Ann Mallough, her mother.
Duncan's father, George, a Catholic from Ireland, married a Scottish Heiress and Duncan attended Upper Canada College. Upon completion, Duncan returned to Scotland with his mother and received his Master's at the University of Edinborough. He returned to Canada after his mother's death and became a master at Upper Canada College, teaching languages, of which he spoke seven… Duncan met Sarah Ann Mallough in London, Ontario and they were married in 1859…He left teaching and became a

bank auditor… upon the arrival of their fourth daughter he toddled unto a boat to Melbourne, Australia where he taught Science and Languages in the University…"

Mary Jane's granddaughter, **Maudie,** my mother, and **Jessie**'s fourth daughter, writes,

"Jessie's mother, Mary Jane Staples, had three sisters. When the fourth was born, her father was outraged because he had no son so left his wife and four daughters and moved to Melbourne, Australia. At that time there was no mother's allowance or welfare, so Mary Jane's mother had to give her children away to relatives who would be willing to bring them up while she worked to support them the best she could. Mary Jane lived with her Aunt Jane Mallough(Fletcher) her mother's sister, in Cardwell township".

Uncle Bill Howell writes about his mother, Mary Jane:

"The Fletcher's had only boys, so a sister was welcomed into the family. The three boys loved Mary Jane as she was much older. William Fletcher died of pneumonia. John was crushed and drowned in the Rousseau River while breaking a log jam. Bob, the youngest was an officer with Lord Strathcona force in the Boer War."

**Maudie** continues:

"In Yearley, Mary Jane, my grandmother, met and married Lorenzo Howell. He was a well-educated man and reasonably well off. Mary Jane did not attend school and could not read or write. It was reported that in situations where she would be expected to read, Lorenzo would say, "Give me that paper, you don't have your glasses with you."

Anything that was lacking, she certainly made up for with kindness, gentleness and understanding. When Lorenzo had a stroke, she nursed him at home until he died in 1929. He couldn't talk at all and his legs were paralyzed. Folks didn't go to hospitals and nursing homes as they do now. My Mom, **Jessie**, stayed down there every night so Grandma could get some rest. My sister, Hester and I did chores for her, bringing in wood and water. Eva couldn't of course because of her condition."

**Jessie's** father, **Lorenzo Howell** (1850-1929) and Mary Jane's husband, was born in Corinth, Township of Bayhem, Elgin County. He learned millwrighting in Pennsylvania, as a teenager, while living with the Best family, his mother's relatives. He had an inborn desire to be a successful lumber and mill operator.

He moved to Tillsonburg and from there, located in Parry Sound District, near the Townline, dividing McMurrich and Stisted townships, under the authority of the Free Grant and Homestead Act in 1875. He made and peddled wooden pumps and dug wells.

In the spring of 1885, he snowshoed to Manitoulin Island, a distance of nearly 80 miles, where he purchased a pair of ponies from the Indians that lived there, as well as harnesses and snowshoes. On the return trip, high winds carried off his remaining supply of hay and he shared his meagre loaf with the ponies until they reached shore where he could get supplies.

With windmill and steam power, he cut shingles and by horse power operating a grist mill and a turning lathe.

A fire destroyed the mill on the Townline. The fire left him practically destitute. His two eldest daughters, Hester and **Jessie**, had to do homework by firelight as there was no money to purchase kerosene for lamps or candles. He wouldn't ask his mother's people for help, but a close neighbour, James Campbell, offered him a waterfall and loaned him $100. With this start, the next mill went up and the demand for lumber and shingles allowed him in a very short time to be in moderate circumstances and free of all debt.

He was able to sell the first property to James Rome and he then moved to Yearley, purchasing the Campbell home in 1895 next to the falls. At this location, he erected a water mill on the Axe River Falls. There he manufactured both lumber and shingles by water power, installing a 75 horse power water turbine. Capturing the energy of falling water through the use of a paddle wheel on the river, he also engineered running water up to the house, a first, for that time.

He was the Post Master for over 20 years and ran a mail stage from Sprucedale to Yearley, thrice weekly. He owned the first automobile in Yearley. He exhibited great interest in all constructions which operated by motor power. At one time he owned 2200 acres of deeded and timbered land. After he passed away no one knew how to operate his mill or the water system and both lay silent from then on.

An article in the "Huntsville Forester Newspaper, dated March 29, 1978" written by Jessie:

"..Another Presbyterian Church, which later became United, ..was the Chalmers United Church, erected on the District Townline between Muskoka and Parry Sound near Yearley. Built of pioneer pine framed by the late Mr. Peters in the year 1887, it was erected by local residents on an acre of cemetery ground donated by the late Mr. and Mrs. Lorenzo Howell of Yearley. The ground had been dedicated a year previously.

In this same cemetery lie the remains of Mr. and Mrs. George Shaw whose pioneer dwelling rested on Lot 24 next to Lorenzo's. They were the grandparents of Lady Peel, better known as Beatrice Lillie, Canadian born, British actress and comedic performer. Her parents, Lucie Ann Shaw and John Lillie were married in the little Stone Church in Ilfracombe. Beatrice and her sister Muriel spent many of their childish and happy holidays with their grandparents as they roamed over the fields."

Years later, Jessie promoted, through informed newspaper articles, the process of reforestation, thus rebuilding and restoring the land that had been gutted by clear-cutting enterprises. She wrote that some of the stumps of the fine pine trees harvested, were three feet in diameter.

"Within the Chalmers Church the inside lining boards were all hand planed and measure 18 to 22 inches wide. In recent times, with considerable repairs needed, the Presbytery reluctantly decided to sell the building rather than let it fall into decay. Mr. and Mrs. Bentley, formerly Mrs. Jessie Howell, daughter of the late Lorenzo Howell, purchased it and the splendid old timbers were used in the construction of a cottage..."

Their eldest daughters, Hester (1882-1897) and **Jessie** (1884-1955), enjoyed helping her father, Lorenzo, while at the mill.

Uncle Bill Howell writes of **Lorenzo**..

"Ren spoke Welsh, German and some of his brothers did also. This was little known by us as his English was fluent." His mother Marion Best was of German descent.

# CHAPTER 8

The children of Lorenzo Howell and Mary Jane Staples:
Hester, **Jessie**, Melbourne, Laurie, Florence, Stanley, Nora, and William.

Hester Howell (1882-1897)
Alex writes about his Aunt Hester's accident in 1897:
This occurred at the Yearley saw mill, not far from the present-day Outdoor Learning Center, operated by the Board of Education.

"Lorenzo stopped the mill to repair something. He told Hester and Jessie and told them he would start it up again as soon as he made the repair. Hester or Jessie responded, but Hester immediately went to repairing something on her own. Hester and Jessie were in sight of each other. Lorenzo was elsewhere. The mill started up, Hester's clothes got caught in one of the belts and tossed her like a rag doll. Jessie couldn't reach her. Jessie ran up the stairs to get Lorenzo to stop the mill as quickly as possible but not quick enough to save Hester. She had serious injuries to one arm and one leg. She was rushed to the hospital. Doctors amputated the leg immediately."

Hester wrote letters home to her "Pa", Lorenzo, Sept. 22, 1897, and Nov. 15, 1897.

These letters were found <u>some 80 years later</u>, in a cardboard tube, in the attic of Jessie and Andrew's family home. The letters provide insight into the ordeal and strength of this young lady.

Hester writes, from the Huntsville Hospital:
"Dear Pa,

I hope you are all right as I am at present. I don't think I'll be home for quite a while yet. The Doctor says that he will have to cut open my arm and cut a piece of the bone out. It won't grow together so there will be a space with no bone at all. The doctor says I will only be laid up for three or four days and that it will soon heal up. I am learning to walk now. Dr Hart says I will be able to walk in a week. I hope I can. Dr Hart has promised that when I can walk out to the buggy that he will take me out for a drive. I hope it won't be long, so if I go, I will want a coat. When I go out now the nurse puts two quilts around me. I would rather have a coat than a shawl. The coat I want will only cost 4 dollars and 25 cents to bring it up. Please don't say no. I have not spent any money for about a month. I am keeping it to help get the coat. I have got that $1.25 that you gave me and the 25 cents from before. I can stand up all alone with my hand on a chair. The shoe maker came yesterday to measure my foot for a shoe. He says he doesn't know how much it will cost. I will get it this week. Why don't you come down to see me now? I expected you Sunday before last and last Sunday and you have not come yet. I have lent my money. I don't know how many times to the Doctor and I lent it again yesterday. I tell them I will have to take interest for it. I would like to know what I am to do about getting my clothes washed. They don't wash the patients' clothing and there are no chances of sending them home and when would I get them again. There is a widow woman with four children and I know her and I am sure I could get her to do them for me. She goes out washing and scrubbing. Her name is Mrs. Scott. She scrubs here sometimes. What will I do? There will be only my chemise, drawers and petties that I think, need to be washed. I don't need any more clothes for a while. I got a letter from Grandma and she says she will try and come down when I go home. I guess that will be all.

From Hester. (continuing)

I got a pamphlet on artificial limbs last night but it doesn't say how much they are. I think I will send away for a catalogue. It says to send away. You don't need to send envelopes or paper for they give them to patients. People have been very kind. I have had 2 peaches for 3 or 4 days and have some yet. I have quite a few crab apples and Mr. Thompson, a man that works for the Doctor, sent over some grapes and peaches. The Salvation Army have been up quite often to see me and I get a war cry every week. Tell Jessie not to forget to send me down quite big piece of shamrock, the pink and white please. Please don't forget. From Hester."

November 15, 1897, Hester writes,
"Dear Pa,
I hope you are well. I am not better yet, but soon to be. My arm pains all the time. Dr Hart thinks he will have to take it off. There is a piece of bone that came out and he says it should not have come out. But don't be alarmed, he is not sure that he will have to take it off yet. Say Pa, I would like it if you could get my leg made soon so when I come home and I want to do something, I can help myself. You could measure my other leg and get it made by it. If you don't get it made, I cannot walk a step without being helped. It would not take long to get it made, I don't think, would it? If Dr. Hart is going to take off my arm, I don't want him to be long about it. Tell Ma I got that ribbon and Mr. Wardell made me a present of it. How did Florence like the apples and grapes and biscuits? Nellie Warren was down to see me yesterday. I got Jessie's post card Saturday night. I hope if Dr. Hart is going to take my arm, he will not probe it or hurt it a lot. Just I have troublesome dreams at night. I think it is just from my arm, for I wake up crying. But I slept a little better last night. I wanted them to get me something to eat for dinner. But they didn't get me anything and I feel so hungry. I guess that will be all. Don't forget to get my leg made for I can't do anything without any leg. You will get this letter on Wednesday and write one and mail it on Friday. I will have it Saturday night. This is all. From Hester"

A letter written Dec. 8, 1897 by S. McMurchy, Huntsville Hospital.

"Dear Mr. Howell,

I have not had time to write you before. Now, I shall try to tell you the little I can about the last days of our little girl. She spoke of all of you a good deal before the arm was amputated. Afterwards she said very little. Her weakness was so great. The arm had pained her a good deal on Thursday and Friday and she said to me a great many times that she hoped the Doctor would take it off. I carried her downstairs to the operating room on Saturday morning. She stood the operation very well and as soon as she recovered from the effects of the chloroform, she asked if her arm was off. I told her it was and she said, "Oh, I am so glad." It was such a relief to her to be rid of it. I carried her upstairs again to her room and all the rest of that day she felt very sick, vomited every little while, but her arm caused her no pain. Sunday, all day she was about the same, could retain no nourishment that we gave her and through the night Sunday, she grew worse. When the nurse came to tell me, I went to her. She had been delirious part of the time. When I got to her, she seemed to know me and said, "Put your arms around me and hug me tight." I did for the last time. After that she was unconscious all the time. When I said you had come, she seemed to partly understand but became queer and dazed right away. In her delirium that afternoon, she kept calling to the home people, not to us. Spoke of her mother and Jessie. She was able to read the post card she got on Saturday night and she also got a letter from one of the nurses who had been here. She got me to read the letter to her as she was tired. She had wanted me to send you a postcard on Saturday morning, telling you that the arm would likely be taken off. We were so busy I could not send it. I was very sorry that you did not see her while she was sensible. Poor little girl. She was so glad to see you when you were here last and talked about you after you went away.

The night after the operation I told her to try to bear it all as well as she could and we would ask Our Heavenly Father to help her.

She said, "I ask Him myself too and He does help me." I am satisfied that our dear Hester is safe with her Savior and you to whom she was so dear, must try to remember what loving tender care she is receiving now. So much better than any of her earthly friends could give her. The piece of lace that was sent with the other things, she made herself. Some more as well, she gave to Nurse McIntyre, who left the hospital about a month ago. I hope you missed nothing I think I sent everything that was left with the lady who brought the note. There are three plants of hers here which we will try to take care of till you come to get them. If there is any other information you want, I shall be glad to give it to you.

Very sincerely your friend,

S. McMurchy, Huntsville Hospital."

Hester Howell passed away due to the mill accident when she was 15 years old.

The article in the Huntsville Forester newspaper read;

"It is our painful task on this occasion to refer you to one of those visitations of Divine Providence which we generally regard as being the most severe that we are called upon to reference in life. Thursday, December 2nd the remains of the late Hester Howell were borne to their last resting place. The funeral was announced to take place at ten o'clock, but shortly after noon friends began to assemble, and when the hour for departure had arrived, a large number of sympathizing friends had gathered from far and near. The cartage proceeded to the Presbyterian Church in the burial ground on the Town Line, where services were held.

Deceased, it will be remembered, met with a severe accident about six months ago and has been undergoing medical treatment, including several severe operations, undergone at the Huntsville Hospital, all of which were endured with bravery which elicited the admiration and love of all those attending upon her. On Monday last, her terrible sufferings were ended by the summons to come up higher and she is now one of those who have gone up out of such tribulation.

Rev. A Chapman, Methodist Minister of this station, conducted the services, enlarging upon the lessons to be learned by these sad events, and in a feeling manner, endeavoured to comfort the bereaved family, who are old residents, highly esteemed by all who know them.

Deceased was fifteen years of age and much loved by old and young."

# CHAPTER 9

**Jessie** (1884-1955), second born to Lorenzo Howell and Mary Jane Staples:

Jessie Howell, married to Andrew Hickling, was mother of Alex, Muriel, Hester, Eva and **Maudie**, as mentioned before, she was an incredible woman.

Post mistress, quilter, rug maker, midwife, undertaker and graveyard attendant, hostess for numerous garden parties, newspaper correspondent, saw mill worker, historian, church secretary, women's institute member, leader in reforestation efforts and last but not least cottage builder. She would also purchase flour, and sugar in bulk, which were delivered by train to Sprucedale. She would then divvy it out, for sale, reasonably, to neighbours, that were unable to afford large purchases.

Her brother, William (Bill) Howell writes,

"She was born June 29, 1884 and was educated in Yearley and on Christmas day,1907, became the bride of Andrew Hickling. She worked at Grunwald Tourist Home in Huntsville, where the men from the sawmill boarded. She also worked for Dr. Howland at the hospital in Huntsville. She had $300 in the bank when she got married, a healthy sum in those days.

She dated Charlie Christianson, Jimmy Beal and Herbert Bentley before choosing to marry Andrew Hickling. Jessie and Andrew must have courted by correspondence as there didn't seem to be any noted courtship. Andrew came home from the lumber camp on a Saturday, dressed up for church on Sunday, had dinner at the Howell home and married Jessie that afternoon. He then returned to the lumber camp that night. He had $3000 in the bank, purchased a one-hundred-acre lot from his father for $400 and on that property Jessie and Andrew built the family home in 1908. After Andrew passed away in 1939, she remained a widow until she married Herbert Bentley of Burk's Falls, in 1949."

She was a very capable individual and nothing seemed to be beyond her.

Edgar Albert Guest writes,
It Couldn't Be Done
Somebody said that it couldn't be done,
But he with a chuckle replied
That "Maybe it couldn't" but he would be one
Who wouldn't say so till, he'd tried,
So, he buckled right in with a trace of a grin
On his face. If he worried, he hid it
He started to sing as he tackled the thing
That couldn't be done, and he did it…..

Of note was Jessie's ingenuity and drive that anything could be done. She, single handedly, built a summer house in front of the family home, for house guests and family that visited. It was large enough to hold two beds and had proper windows and door. As a child, I, along with my sisters and brother would play there and would fight over who could be in Aunt Eva's wheelchair, left in the summer house, which Aunt Eva had used as a child.

When the Chalmers Church on the Townline was sold, Jessie purchased all the lumber and proceeded to build a third structure, her cottage on their property. Her second husband, Herb Bentley helped with its completion. This building still stands, while the homestead next door, is in disrepair and likely will need to be demolished in the near future.

Both Jessie and her first husband, Andrew died of stomach cancer at the ages of 71 and 70, respectively.

# CHAPTER 10

Melbourne Howell (1886-1952):

Uncle Alex writes about his Uncle Melbourne, third child of Lorenzo Howell and Mary Jane Staples, (named Melbourne as that was where Mary Jane's father lived.),

"He was quite comical and entertaining prior to 1914. He worked in the sawmill a few years, joining the army when he was about 20 years of age. He wrote home every two weeks regularly. Every letter was addressed, "Dear Ma, Jessie and the rest." My mother, Jessie, answered all the letters, since Grandma couldn't write. War ended in 1918 but he waited nearly two years in England, before he could get a boat home. The army had a job for him when he got home and he met a local girl, Mabel Smith (1900-1985), from Ilfracombe. They were married in 1920.

Melbourne (1886-1952) spent five years in the Canadian Army and ten years at a Toronto factory, making aluminum frying pans. They lived in Swansea, Toronto. This lasted until every home had at least one aluminum frying pan. He got laid off and never really got another job. It was 1930. The Depression was on and no one could get a job, but he struggled along, until he died in 1952. I think he had about seven children but I never got to know them."

Laurie Howell (1888-1889) There is no record of her short life.

Florence Howell (1892-1955):

Uncle Bill Howell writes about Florence,

"Florence had the brains, the looks and was always the student in the family becoming a teacher at the age of 18. She married Einar Einarson, and lived in Rousseau. She and her father wrote to Wales before her marriage and they gleaned some information about the Howell family. It involved a crest or coat of arms, which was probably for Welch patriotism or resistance to English rule. Three Howells were imprisoned in England and later deported as potential revolutionaries around the first of the 17th century. The Howell name had only one "l" until they moved to the United States, settling near Bloomington, Indiana.

Florence lost her eldest son, at the age of 24, when he was shot down over Singapore at the first of the war. Married at the time, he didn't get to see his only child. Florence's husband, Einar, died quite young and she studied and obtained her second teaching certification at the age of 52.

Stanley Howell (1894-1897) There is no known record regarding Stanley's short life.

Nora Howell (1899-1942)

Nora was the seventh of eight children born to Lorenzo and Mary Jane Staples.

As a young child she was very good at poetry, however school was not her strength. At the age of 18, she went to work at Psychiatric Hospital at 999 Queen Street East in Toronto. It was there that she contracted tuberculosis. She was living with Melbourne, her brother, at the time and shared a room with their daughter, Dorothy. Unfortunately, Dorothy also fell victim to the sickness and died very young. The family devastated with the death of their daughter, told

Nora that she was no longer able to live with them. She moved to the hospital in Gravenhurst where she died.

It is believed that Nora never married and financially helped the family her entire life. She enjoyed writing poetry and poking fun at family members. A happy sort and loved by all.

# CHAPTER 11

William Howell (1904-1986), a large contributor to the family story:
Last, but by no means least, the youngest child of Lorenzo and Mary Jane was William Howell, or Bill, more commonly known. In his later years, he became a family historian and researched many avenues tracing the paths the Howell name, found both in Canada and the US. He married a school teacher, Evelyn M. Hawn and lived in Burk's Falls. As a young man, he had the reputation of being somewhat of a scoundrel.

Uncle Alex writes about his Uncle Bill, only 5 years his senior,
"My first memories of Willie would be when I was about 4 and I thought he was the most wonderful person in the world. One of the reasons for this was due to the fact that, Willie, Nora and Grandma each contributed 25 cents toward buying me a 75cent hand sleigh for Christmas. When I was 5 (1914), Grandpa Howell bought his first model T and Willie explained to me how a differential worked. When I was about 9, Willie bought a 6x6 white tent and we pitched it on the lawn and Willie and I slept in it in the summertime for several years. Willie was always there. When he was quite young perhaps 11 or 12, he drove taxi for Tom Rowe of Sprucedale, so of course he lived in Sprucedale during this period.
Willie passed his High School Entrance at 12 years of age, then went to Toronto to live with his older brother, Melbourne, and go to High School.

Melbourne said he couldn't get him to stay in school and Grandpa Howell made several trips to try to persuade him to stick with school but he wasn't interested at all. He eventually quit school completely and got a job selling newspapers. This was fairly successful for a while until he started smoking and stealing cigarettes, which got him in trouble with the police. A policeman, Davey Dunn took an interest in Willie and sensing there would be trouble in the future, if Willie was to stay in the city, so he told him to leave Toronto and never come back.

He came back to Yearley, when he was 16. I believe that one of his main aims in life was to be liked by people, all people, especially girls his own age. In this, I believe his success was outstanding. He dated Evelyn Smith and she had two children, suspected of being Willie's.

He had limited tolerance for the opinions of others that differed from his and when he was drinking, this erupted violently. When I was 17, we went to Alberta together on the harvest excursion. It was during this experience, I decided alcohol wasn't such a good idea. He was co-operative to work, but evenings seemed to bug him. Saving money never crossed his mind. His interest was, "Let's draw some money from the boss and walk into town." I went with him once or twice but he sometimes went alone. He wasn't disagreeable yet at that point. That started when he was about 24.

Willie lived with Grandma Howell from the time Grandpa died in 1929 till 1935 when she passed. Willie had two new cars during this period and dressed very well. When she died Melbourne was the executor, while she was alive, Willie would get her to sign checks for various purposes. Grandma had no education and she didn't know what she was signing. By 1935 there was no money left to distribute. Jessie, wanted Melbourne to sue Willie for fraud. By this time Melbourne was caught up in the Depression and had no money to even engage a lawyer, so he refused. He told Jessie, Mom, "I'll sue if you come up with the money." Mom said, "No, the will says you are the executor and that's your job." Of course, they both knew Willie wouldn't have any money and the best one could hope for would be to send him to jail. No money in that."

Willie married Evelyn Hawn in 1939 and had one daughter, Sylvia, a very talented violinist. Evelyn taught school and completed her degree at Queen's University and continued with post graduate studies at York University. She was a respected member in the community of Burk's Falls and was a member of the Board of Education for the District for many years.

Uncle Alex continues,

"Probably the most constructive thing Willie did was to build the house for Evelyn. It's nice that she has her own house to live in and it is nice that he was able to contribute toward that in his own way."

# CHAPTER 12

Our parents: Florence **Maude** Hickling (1920-2003) and Robert Soper (1917-2001). There were five children born in this union, Sylvia (1941), Robert (Bob) (1943), Maryne (1945-2016), Carolyn (1946) and Mark (1965)

Our father, Robert Soper or Bob, was dedicated to his family, an avid sailor, Masonic lodge member, organist at the church for years and seemed to be able to fix anything. His ancestry is traced in "A British Immigrant's Story" published in 2021.

Mom's first name was Florence, however, as a child she was unable to pronounce it so "Maude" became the norm.

Dad moved north with Grandma and Grandad Soper, in 1933 and had occasions at different social events to cross paths with Mom. The deciding night was at a dance at Sunnyside Park in Toronto. Mom was engaged to someone else, up north, and was enjoying a night out, while visiting Aunt Hester, in the city. Dad asked Mom to dance and when together were spotted by Aunt Minnie, from Dad's side. Having a sharp eye, she spotted the engagement ring and assuming that they were a couple, congratulated them and asked them if they had set a date. Dad, very cool, responded, "Sometime in the fall." Mom made a change in her plans and as she said to me, "I think I made the right choice."

Our Mom was the greatest in so many ways it is difficult to know where to begin. She instilled in us the love of reading. Living at the farm, before hydro, by coal oil lamp, I can recall curled up near her, listening to her read to the four of us, before going to bed. Laura Ingalls' Little House on The Prairie, My Friend Flicka, Thunderhead, Lassie, Anne of Green Gables and of course all the Christopher Robin Stories by A.A. Milne, Maggie Muggins, Tom Sawyer, Huckleberry Finn, the list goes on and on.

From our bedrooms upstairs, we could hear the sound of the rocking of the pedal of the sewing machine as she made new flannelette pajamas for each of us for Christmas and clothes for our dolls.

Memories such as eating freshly baked bread with butter, upon our arrival home, getting off the school bus. After we got hydro in the house and Grandad Soper purchased a television for us in the 50's, the rules of no tv except for weekends were accepted, reluctantly. Week nights were for school work.

Neighbours would come over and pulling out the couch and placing chairs behind it, making room for all, we would watch, the vitally important, "Hockey Night in Canada" with Foster Hewitt. Following the game, we all enjoyed hot chocolate and the friendship of Fordes, the O'Hallorans and the Blacks.

Sometimes we would have a music night with my brother, Bob on the violin, Dad on the piano and Steve Black on the guitar, as we sang along. On Sundays the O'Hallorans, Blacks and Sopers would gather and have services in our home thankful for the gift of friends and family.

During the week, in winter months, Mom would call all four of us at about 8:30 to close our books and put on our hats and coats to go for a walk down the long swamp, before bed. She always said the fresh air would help us remember our assignments and would provide the fresh air that was necessary for a wonderful, restful sleep.

We all felt loved and part of an effort to get by. Helping with piling and bringing in wood, planting, digging and picking up potatoes, shoveling snow, washing, ironing, baking and cleaning house.

We had a barrel churn with a wooden handle to rock back and forth as the barrel made complete rotations within the framework. There was a cork plug that one would have to open from time to time to release the gases created by the turning. On one occasion this releasing part was not done properly and the cork blew and buttermilk was catapulted across the walls and ceiling in quite a glorious display. Not a happy occasion for all on clean up duty that day.

The clumps of butter produced within this churn, Mom would scoop out and carefully pat it and work it until all the whey had been squeezed out of it. She then placed the wad of butter in a wooden frame that resembled a miter saw frame of today. Thus, the butter took on its square shape, cut in appropriate sizes, for the parchment paper, used to wrap each pound for storage. Many good memories. I admired her deftness with the process as it was an acquired skill for sure.

We had a milk separator which yielded the cream from one spout and skim milk from the lower spout. The cream was poured into sterilized metal cream cans and ready for sale. These full metal cream cans were taken to the Emsdale train station for shipment to the Huntsville Dairy. We were raised drinking only skim milk and I have never been able to handle the thickness of whole milk to this day.

One Saturday, Sylvia, Maryne and I were baking cookies in the wood stove, Mom was not at home. We realized that the chimney was on fire. We were in a panic. We were able to douse the fire in the stove, with baking soda and water, however we could still hear the roar of the fire in the chimney. We were in a bit of a panic since the roof was made of cedar shingles. Thinking that more baking soda and water was the needed response, I got up on the roof and Sylvia and Maryne would pass the mixture for me, to pour down the chimney. I came close to meeting my Maker as I, at the last minute realized I would have run into the hydro lines that crossed the roof near the chimney. Close call…Here to tell the tale…

Mom had many special visits with our cousins Shirley and Nancy, Hester's daughters. These were filled with laughter and long talks into the night.

Mom made grandchildren and great grandchildren feel very special and she is well remembered for her Gramma hugs. The kind of hug that takes your breath away.

Growing up on a farm gave us the sense of complete freedom. We roamed the forest, building forts, creating fantasies in our play together. Family dogs followed us around on our escapades at the beaver pond. We had special places to explore and express our ideas and joy.

As children on the farm, we would gather around the kitchen table, that had been covered with paper and watch our father clean and gut the carcass of a chicken, in preparation for the next day's dinner meal. He would pull out the insides and we, in wonderment, had a very good lesson on anatomy. He was a very patient man and provided explanations to our never-ending questions.

I recall the exciting night that the tractor broke partially through the ice back at the beaver pond and all the neighbours were called to winch it out. That was quite an experience. Group effort, ingenuity and problem solving at work, giving us an excellent example of that which drove our grandmother, Jessie, and others' response to "it couldn't be done". Those opportunities teach such valuable lessons for the life that follows.

We had a telephone on a party line that worked sometimes. Everyone knew what was going on as one could not tell if someone else had picked up the line and was listening in. Long distance calls had to be routed through a phone operator's switch board. We have come a long way in 60 years.

# CHAPTER 13

The children of Florence Maude Hickling and Robert Soper: Sylvia, Bob, Maryne, Carolyn and Mark.

Sylvia Maude (1941):

Mom told me about one of Sylvia's earliest duties in caring for her siblings. Sylvia liked to go to Sunday school when they lived Port Stanley. Sylvia would have been four and Bob would have been two years of age.

Bob decided he wanted to go with his sister to church, so Mom walked them to the church, promising to return and walk them back afterward.

With the husbands away, in the Air Force, the wives would take turns preparing meals for their families, taking alternate days and this particular day, it was Mom's turn.

Upon entering the church, the loud organ music scared Bob and he was led by Sylvia, crying, out of the church. An hour later, Mom recalled seeing the sorrowful pair sitting on the church steps, Sylvia with her arm around her brother, dutifully waiting for Mom's return.

Sylvia, like the rest of us had/has a mind of her own. While living in Port Stanley, first, she took to running away to play, in the sand, down by the water. The police brought her home a number of times saying, "Here is your child again." Later, at the age of 4, she assisted her brother, Bob, aged 2, escape his playpen to accompany her on her travels away from home.

Since Sylvia was quite an escape artist, Mom had to relent to tying them to the clothes line in the back yard. Don't think that would be allowed today.

Sylvia recalls her duties being, carrying the diaper bag, whenever they went anywhere. Having three younger siblings must have been a chore.

Five years older than I, Sylvia could not understand why her parents had to go to town on such a stormy night in November, the night of I was born.

Sylvia left the farm with plans of being a city girl. She worked in a bank for a number of years and Maryne and I, being in high school, really enjoyed weekends in the city, with our elder sister.

She purchased our first modern record player and 78's and 45's to go along with it. She also purchased a large dining room table and chairs for our parents, wonderful examples of her generous heart.

Sylvia married Ed Maki and they raised four wonderful children, Bill, Jim, Andy and Nancy on a farm north of Sprucedale. City life was over...

She received certification to work with Developmentally Handicapped, working with them locally, for a number of years. She, also very efficiently, managed the books for Ed's businesses and farming endeavours. She is the family encyclopedia of information, remembering everything.

Still a risk taker, while visiting her not long ago, she would drive the half ton truck to the barn to help with the chores and since the windshield was completely frosted over, Sylvia gave me a frightful trip, as she went all the way looking out the side window at the snowbank, that being her gauge reassuring her that we were on the road. Fortunately, no traffic at that time of the morning...

Robert Douglas (Bob) (1943):

He was the most patient brother anyone could have, considering growing up with three sisters.

He was always an entrepreneur, raising pigs, cattle, chickens, as well as peeling pulpwood and pruning trees along with the rest of us.

He would tap the many maples up the hill from our farm house and boil the sap down in a large black iron pot. We spent many hours sitting by that fire, singing songs as he strummed along.

The final boiling was done on the kitchen stove and made the house smell delicious. Mom said that was the reason she had to wallpaper so frequently. The sticky walls needed to be refreshed with a new cover.

Bob played the violin, piano, banjo, mandolin and guitar.

He was particularly good at imitating a favorite, Johnny Cash.

Having a musical talent, he wanted to improve his violin skills and went to the classical violin teacher in Burk's Falls and asked if she would teach him how to play proper fiddle music, "not classical stuff", as he put it. She agreed and the night of the music concert at the High School, he was the last on the program. The audience had likely had their fill of the classics and when Bob started to play, he got a standing ovation and was compelled to play an encore. Quite a highlight for him.

I remember him putting on the big black 78's, vinyl records, on the old gramma phone. This fiddle music, he played over and over until he could play right along with each of them.

We had many enjoyable evenings growing up with Dad on the piano and Bob playing violin, all the old favorites.

Being somewhat cagey, I recall him persuading me that nickels were worth more than dimes since they were bigger. Mom caught him making an exchange with me and that put an end to that.

Bob completed a Bachelor of Science Degree at the University of Guelph. He played in a band at the university and was, at times, sidetracked by billiards. He enjoyed various occupations, however raising beef cattle, I think was closest to his heart.

Maryne June (1945-2016):
An excellent student, she skipped two grades, 3 to 4 and 7 to

8, in elementary school, and entered Teacher's College at the age of 16. While she was teaching, she always felt nervous going to staff functions, afraid they would ask for ID. The entry age at the time was 21 and she was well under that. Her first class was a group of 40 grade 2 students, quite a feat for an 18-year-old, in a school on Kingston Road in Toronto.

She married Rick Trask and followed his dreams, living in Alberta, British Colombia, various places in Ontario and when she finally returned to Muskoka, she said no to his plan of moving to Newfoundland. She raised three sons, Brad, Jayson and Chad.

With a husband, home and three sons to care for, she completed her Bachelor's degree by correspondence through Western University, listening to tapes of lectures while driving to and from work.

She taught Junior and Senior Kindergarten in Dorset. When she was leaving the school in Dorset, the Principal held an assembly for the students to say goodbye. He asked for those that had had her for a teacher to raise their hands. Seeing a multitude of hands, he changed his request to, "How many have not had Mrs. Trask as their teacher?" Those numbers were few. She definitely had an impact within the community. Students exited her kindergarten class with the ability to read.

I was blessed to overhear two young girls talking, in the waiting room at the Doctor's office in Huntsville, where I, as her executor, was scheduled to meet with him, following her passing. The one girl said to the other. "Did you hear that Mrs. Trask passed away?" The response was, "No I hadn't, shame, she was one of the good ones." She made a difference.

During her last years of teaching, after obtaining additional Special Education qualifications, at the Brantford School for the Blind, she was a Resource Teacher for Limited Vision and Blind students throughout the district. She shared with me a conversation she had with one of those special individuals.

The little girl, having very limited vision, asked Maryne what wrinkles were. She told her that as people age, the skin changes and isn't as smooth as when you are young. The child thought about it and in pure innocence asked, "Mrs. Trask, do you have any wrinkles?" Maryne said that she was so tempted to say no, however her honest nature required her to tell the truth regarding the presence of wrinkles on her face. She could have continued the illusion of youth, but thought better of it.

Her joy during her later years were her granddaughters, Jasmine, Teagan, Tori and Madison.

Unfortunately, she succumbed to pancreatic cancer and passed away in 2016. In her last days, since cancer does not affect the quality of the eyes, the doctor asked her if she might consider organ donation. Without any hesitation, she said, "Of course". Therefore, we know she gave sight to many others after she departed. She is greatly missed.

Carolyn Marie (1946):

I remember being a challenge for our Mother, and spent considerable time sitting behind the kitchen door, in time out. Being a determined sort, I tended to step out of line on occasion and I recall Mom sitting me down and asking me with comforting tones, "What did you learn from that?" That took the fear away from being reprimanded and helped one consider a different course of action.

I am forever grateful to her for saving me from drowning when I was 8. Living in Pakesley, near Parry Sound, when Dad worked for Lands and Forests, we all went down to the falls past the one room school house.

Bob and his buddy, Murray Styles, were fishing and we girls had the idea of washing our hair in the river. Maryne and Sylvia found a safe spot where they could lay on a rock that protruded out into the water. Not to be outdone by my sisters, I laid down on a sloping rock which was slippery and in I went, head first, just like an otter. I didn't recall anything, until afterwards sputtering, having been pulled out of the river by Mom. It was quite a feat since she didn't know how to swim and her instinct took over and she jumped in after me, saving my life.

We attended, while there, a one room school house, now acknowledging that, I feel I lived through a time warp. There were two of us in Grade 3, Joyce Watts and myself, sharing a wide desk with a long bench seat that flipped up in the event we were asked to stand. We copied copious notes off the blackboard, overheard lessons of the previous and future grades. We were introduced to straight pens that we dipped into the glass inkwells on the right-hand upper corner of each space. Ball point pens were such an improvement.

Four of the students arrived by train each morning. There were perhaps 15 students in all. The teacher lived in a small room at the back of the classroom and there was a pot-bellied stove that belched out the heat on colder days. The teacher filled her non-teaching hours working in a wonderful garden beside the school house and from time to time would provide everyone with a lesson or two on gardening. It was another enriching experience, cherished in my memory.

I followed my sister's path and entered the teaching profession. Initially in elementary schools over a period of 20 years. I held various positions in Primary and Special Education, Early Childhood Education, Resource, Student Assessment, Consultant, enjoying the last 13 years of my teaching career in a Secondary School in Niagara, all while completing Bachelor of Arts, followed by Master's and Doctoral degrees in Education, through part time studies.

My husband, Frank Miehle, of German descent enriched our experiences with travel to Europe, participation at the German Canadian Club, soccer playing and coaching, tournaments, hockey, golf excursions. Together, we raised his two children, Frank Jr. and Susan. All activities broadened our circle of friends and brought much happiness. Frank passed away in 2019, after a lengthy battle with Alzheimer's.

After the passing of my husband, I had a serious talk with myself and decided, I was the only one that could choose how I would proceed, make the best of things or give up. He would want me to go on and I know he is just a whisper away.

All experiences enrich our lives and as Forest Gump put it, "Life is a box of chocolates, you never know what you are going to get."

All experiences provide opportunities to grow, meet new people and watch life unfold before us. Wouldn't have missed any of it.

Mark Andrew (1965).

Mark arrived in 1965, he was the surprise child. Mom was 45 when he was born and he filled the empty nest, as all of his siblings were off married, working or beginning their studies.

His first years, they lived at the Provincial Girl Guide Camp, where Dad was employed doing maintenance on all buildings, and equipment.

He, like his siblings, had a mind of his own, early in life, while in Canadian Tire, he was adamant about what he wanted and Mom, totally frustrated and tired of trying to manage such a determined child, went to customer service and asked them to page Dad and she left the building. The announcement was "Will Mr. Soper please come to Customer Service to pick up his son."

Frank and I visited during the winter and after enjoying a ride on the snowmobiles, Mark proceeded to explain to both of us how the internal combustion engine worked. He was perhaps 6 years old at the time. He soaked up information like a sponge. It was so wonderful that both Mom and Dad had the time and energy to guide this wonderful soul.

Mark belonged to air cadets and obtained his glider pilot's license and even got Mom up in the glider with him for a ride. Mom said that she had misgivings once strapped in and questioned her own sanity. She said, "I sat and watched him so many times it seemed that it was an ok thing to do."

Quite successful scholastically, he entered the navy out of High

School, completed a degree in Electrical Engineering, served at sea, in the Ojibway submarine, and upon his retirement, held the rank of Lieutenant Commander. He then moved on and at time of writing, is a Senior Manager with Fleetway Marine Engineering, located in Halifax. His jovial laugh is a joy to hear and coupled with his bear hugs, one always knows they are loved.

# CHAPTER 14

A poem that our Mother requested be read at our father's funeral and was repeated again for her, is as follows:

**How Do You Live Your Dash?**
I read of a man who stood to speak
At the funeral of a friend
He referred to the dates on her tombstone
From the beginning .....to the end

He noted that first came her date of birth
And spoke of the following date with tears.
But he said what mattered most of all
Was the dash between the years.

For that dash represents all the time
That she spent alive on earth
And now only those who loved her
Know what that little line is worth.

For it matters not, how much we own
The cars.. the house ..the cash
What matters is how we live and love
And how we spend our dash.

So think about this long and hard...
Are there things you'd like to change?
For you never know how much time is left,
That can still be rearranged.

If we could just slow down enough
To consider what's true and real,
And always try to understand
The way other people feel.

And be less quick to anger,
And show appreciation more
And love the people in our lives
Like we've never loved before.

If we treat each other with respect,
And more often wear a smile..
Remembering that this special dash
Might only last a little while.

So, when your eulogy's being read
With your life's actions to rehash..
Would you be proud of the things they say
About how you spent your dash?

Author Unknown.

As Abraham-Hicks writes: The basis of life is freedom, the purpose of life is joy and the result of life is growth.

Tracing the paths of our ancestry fills one with gratitude. They experienced heart breaking loss of loved ones and "carried on".

It is with awe that one can sense their watching and encouraging souls, overseeing our lives, as each unfolds. I believe life is eternal and we are composites of all that has gone before. Their DNA is part of all of us. Each of us is blessed to carry them with us. One may have their grandfather's nose on their face. A link with the past. A link with the strength, courage, fortitude, determination, creativity and faith carries each of us forward.

Life is a gift to be treasured.

I have appended a collection of family pictures that will put faces on the pages that have gone before.

The Alexander Hickling Homestead of Alexander and Catharine

Catharine McNabb(1846-1923), Mabel(1886-1928),
Maude(1881-1965), **Andrew**(1869-1939), Alexander(1840-1925)
Absent from photo: son John Henry(1867-1940)

Lorenzo Howell(1850-1929) and
Mary Jane Staples(1861-1934)

Three of Lorenzo and Mary Jane's children:
**Jessie**(1884-1955-) Hester(1882-1897) and Melbourne(1886-1952)

The Lorenzo Howell family:

Florence(1892-1955), **Jessie**(1884-1955),Melbourne(1886-1952)
Lorenzo(1850-1929), William(1904-1986),Mary Jane(1861-1934),
Nora(1894-1942)

Jessie Howell and Andrew Hickling married 1907

Muriel, Andrew(Dad), Jessie(Mom), Alex,
Grandma Howell(Mary Jane), Eva, Hester,
Grandpa Howell(Lorenzo), Maude

Lorenzo Howell family
1912 Buick

Jessie and Andrew Hickling
Alex, Muriel, Hester, Eva, Mau
Their 1925 Star.

Jessie and Andrew Hickling 25th Wedding Anniversary

Jessie and Andrew Hickling family
Labour Day 1922

Jessie and Andrew (back)
Alex, Muriel, Hester, Eva, Maude
1934

Hickling Home 1941

## Yesterday's family car

A drive in the family car has been a popular outing for years. This 1912 McLaughlin-Buick was owned by Lorenzo Howell. Sitting beside Mr. Howell is his son Bill, now of Burks Falls. The McLaughlin-Buick was a right-hand drive car with the gearshift and emergency brake on the outside. The car also had features like kerosene parking lights and acetylene headlights. The car had to be entered from the left side because of the position of the spare tire.

Logging Enterprise

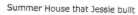

Grandpa Lorenzo Howell's Snow Machine

Summer House that Jessie built

Uncle Alex aka Jack Henry

His home on Bronte Road, Oakville

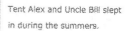

Tent Alex and Uncle Bill slept
in during the summers.

*Mrs. Hickling and her daughter Hester with a rug completed last summer.*

*Rugs that are sure to catch the eye of the tourist.*

Jessie's hooked rugs.

Sylvia, Grandma (Jessie) and Maude

Summer of 1941

*Totally different but equally interesting are these two designs.*

Maudie Hickling and Robert Soper Wedding 1939

Mom, Sylvia and Bob

The four of us, Sylvia, Bob, Maryne and Carolyn

One roomed school house we attended in 1954.

Farm, former Fox Farm.

Dad, Mom, Grandma Soper, Sylvia,
Grandad Soper, Bob, Maryne, Carolyn

Carolyn, Sylvia, Maryne

Grandad Soper, Carolyn, Maryne, Mark, Sylvia, Bob
Mom and Dad

Back row: Mark, Mom, Nancy, Bob, Shirley
Front row: Sylvia, Carolyn, Maryne

Aunt Hester, Maudie's sister and
Mother of Nancy and Shirley Herckimer

The story began with my father's funeral,

Here he is sailing off into the sunset.

On our parents' tombstone in St. Paul's Cemetery, Sprucedale,

It reads: **Smooth Sailing Home.**

Printed in the United States
by Baker & Taylor Publisher Services